HALLELUJAH SCIENCE

Kelli Stevens Kane

SPUYTEN DUYVIL
New York City

© 2020 Kelli Stevens Kane
ISBN 978-1-952419-37-9

Library of Congress Cataloging-in-Publication Data

Names: Kane, Kelli Stevens, author.
Title: Hallelujah science / Kelli Stevens Kane.
Description: New York City : Spuyten Duyvil, [2020] |
Identifiers: LCCN 2020044152 | ISBN 9781952419379 (paperback)
Subjects: LCGFT: Poetry.
Classification: LCC PS3611.A5465 H35 2020 | DDC 811/.6--dc23
LC record available at https://lccn.loc.gov/2020044152

for my parents
AR and EK Stevens

contents

(9) it's nighttime

(42) welcome brain to

(63) these dreams

(35) of course

(60) I had no idea

(56) there are bugs

(40) when I die

(10) when I was

(76) trying to fall asleep

(4) the door slams

(1) arms float

(65) seventeen sisters

(14) shooting

(45) the shadows

(11) if I had

(19) somebody

(85) inside

(18) if I could

(55) close your

(51) chimney

(74) take the lid off

(84) my father

(44) the wind

(15) if

(16) I check

(86) below my sky

(62) I bet

(30) I was dreaming

(48) several sorts of

(70) everyone

(43) if I keep my feet

(31) I don't want to

(5) give it to the pillow

(67) spring rain

(50) the urban waterfall

(71) a swarm of 7,000 bees

(83) it's been too long since

(7) doors open

(82) terrible boy

(81) tell the fire

(61) I like

(75) scratching

(73) all the visitors

(22) if I could

(23) myself

(64) it's okay

(27) there are big ovals

(59) she is

(37) turning

(66) I cut a record

(9)

It's nighttime
when the sickness spreads out
when the cramps grip tighter
when the lost souls of earlier dead encircle me
and blow ancient germs in my face.
I am miserable
my feet are cold
and I want to be alone.
"That's what we wanted too"
chant the souls
blowing in circles.

(42)

welcome brain
to the last moments before sleep.
drugged with fatigue
I slide my words up and down
and my hot hands catch odd associations on paper.
I'm losing contact with the little people
the ones who live in radios and sing.
my face red with upstairs
running

(63)

these dreams I will carry with me
like waves in the air above heat or gasoline

awake in this flaunted house
all kinds of spirit guests walk through

and they'll just have to watch me eat
because I'm not running a restaurant for the dead.

they can do like we did in preschool
and hand each other pretend food:

air biscuits, invisible hamburgers,
and double scoops of nothing.

I hunger for these dreams
I draw one in, and she curls up

pondering my stomach
tasting womb, deciding nothing

(35)

Of course everything revolves around me—
the moon, the stars, the grocery clerks.
Picture me higher than the clouds,
orchestrating lightning flashes.
Who here knows about science?
I'm not talking about beakers and Bunsen burners.
I'm talking about hallelujah science.
Seashell and fossil science.
Look-out-the-window collision science.
Too many people bother me.
I ought to cook them in soup.

(60)

I had no idea I was this late
the invisible shadows of nighttime swallowed
and hicked me up.

I had no idea I was this early
the deadline is still years away
and there is no better crime than the present.

I had no idea I was this black
the ink from my pen blends like lotion
into skin.

I had no idea I was this white
the blank paper swallows and I am invisible
the poem, written, stares.

(56)

there are bugs in the confessional listening to every word I am saying
the bugs are bugged
so you can hear tapes of everything I don't want you to hear
and submit them as evidence that I'm cheating on myself
wasting time
instead of buying it
a necklace
and wearing it

(40)

When I die
I will miss the dark green shape of ivy
and I will miss bark chips.
When I die
I will miss the sound of any living creatures breathing,
the texture of oatmeal,
and the sound of a volleyball being punched into the sky.
When I die
I will miss indentations left on noses from eyeglasses,
the shrinking voice of a child
speeding away on a bicycle
singing *The Jeffersons* theme song,
and leaning from side to side on my bike
making sine waves on cement.
When I die
I will miss yogurt
and thinking about active yogurt cultures and being
multicultural in every spoonful,
the feeling of throwing sticks into water
and watching them drown,
the feeling of sitting on a hot car seat in shorts,
touching a hot steering wheel,
and starting to drive.
When I die
I will miss searching the house
scared to find the cause of a sound never before heard,
the feeling of realizing an ant is crawling across my skin,
and the waking up of every cell when, midday,
I remember a dream.
I will miss shin splints and peeling the skin off steamed yams.
I will miss swimming and chlorine eyes.
When I die
I will miss the feeling of weight,

the smell of dirt from above, and
the mystery of hidden roots
that sew the soil together,
when I die.

(10)

when I was five
I used to rise up out of myself and watch me from behind.
I told my mama,
and she stayed calm.
I told my mama,
and she let me double.

(76)

Trying to fall asleep here is as easy as
relaxing in a doorway during an earthquake.

I am a human X marking the spot
between this world and the next.

No matter where I am,
I'm in the middle of something,

in the middle
of something
lost.

(4)

the door slams
and the house is mine.
I rule from the couch
directing orchestras of dead sons
rehearsing for my funeral.

(1)

arms float as wings
legs dangle as anemone

fingers leave jet trails
toes drag through mud

everything
is taller
lasts longer
is slower
moves softer

cradle me
treetop me
baby me
fall

(65)

seventeen sisters
cling to my pelvis.
one of them
scratched my concept out.

she didn't do it.
no one did.
it's impossible.

(14)

shooting flesh targets
with real guns
throwing rocks into thick windows
lighting matches under white curtains
ripping holes in good clothes
tearing leaves off live plants
puncturing tires
punishing liars
this time of the month
I know you're here

(45)

The shadows have guns and the shapes that make them go undetected. The guns are filled with black holes. Ready to fight back with my finger and thumb gun, I shoot a fake bullet through the window and destroy one ray of the sun. The shadows only get bigger. I try to peel them off with my fingernails, but they won't come loose. I shine a flashlight into them, but I only hear laughing. "Up here," says the sun, "shine it on me!" So I do and the sun laughs harder. "Thanks for the light," it says, as the shadows stick their guns in my back and darkness pours through me like rivers of cold blood.

(11)

if I had a child now
I'd wish I didn't

(19)

somebody should come home soon
and fix me toast
and keep me company.
I'll open a window and play with the wind

(85)

inside this fever
is a waterproof garden
growing seeds
that cannot sprout
unless you stop thinking

(18)

if I could put my head aside
I would twist it like a thermos lid
and pour out all the hot blood
and broken glass
and poison applesauce
and leave me standing

(55)

close your eyes
and stare at the sun
see the particles
floating
around the bright red Jupiter of your eyeball.
which one will be yours
they are waiting
to be born.

(51)

chimney smoke and fog
look like relatives
the mama is the chimney
cranking out ghost babies
that become the fog

(74)

take the lid off the blender while blending
and know that a splatter is pending

(84)

my father
juggles eggs
and one time
the ceiling caught one.
the yellow yolk
landed
laughing.

(44)

the wind blew my house down
so I moved into a sailboat
the wind messed my hair up
so I cut it all off
the wind made my eyes water
so I took up a collection for the sea
the wind threw the clouds out
so I threw wet cotton balls on my ceiling
the wind raised my skirt up
so I mooned it and got arrested
there was no wind in jail

(86)

below my sky
small leaks allow
lost souls to find family
I poke more holes

(62)

I bet if you want anything it's to be tall
like hot apple cider wants to be cold
carbonated water wants to be plain
and good milk wants to go bad.
ice wants to be water
and I can't seem to lie still.
I crawl on my knees
trying to make eye contact
with shortbread.

(30)

I was dreaming about making clay eggs
and I missed some deadline to enter some competition
and when the dream hatched I was bleeding
missing the dead, or those lining up to become alive

(48)

several sorts of socks work well with woolen underwear

(70)

everyone is walking
everyone is walking
everyone is walking
on the road that I am.

(43)

if I keep my feet up
wings will sprout out the sides
and my baby toes will give birth to peanuts.
if I keep my feet up
my knees will stare at my eyeballs
and my sunblock will give birth to a pirate eye patch.
if I keep my feet up
my eyes will be sewn together by lashes
and my lack of sight will give birth
to a better sense of taste
if I keep my feet up.

(31)

I don't want to get up
because gravity will pull
my walls down
they are collapsing
but if I lie still
they can be bathwater
unaware of the drain

(5)

give it to the pillow girl
give it to the pillow
all the belly ache
all the fever
all the cramps
all the blood
please release
I already know

there is no child.

(67)

spring rain falls silently
passive aggressive bitch

(50)

the urban waterfall is
a stream of cars rolling downhill
each engine driving a droplet of car water.
you must pretend you live by a river
you must pretend
the liquid is real

(71)

a swarm of 7,000 bees
mow my neighbor's front lawn

(83)

It's been too long since the last earthquake.
I jump up and down trying to start something.
The glasses in the cabinet clink together like wind chimes.
I can hear them. Nothing breaks.

It's been too long since the last earthquake.
The desk vibrates when a bus goes by.
I jump up and down trying to start something.
The landlord pounds to say quit it.

My dad called me "the instigator"
because I used to tell my mom on him
for waving to women and eating fast food.
Now I'm on to bigger things.

In my dreams, when I jump up and down trying to start something,
buildings leap up into the sky
and the holes they used to stand in
say AAAAAAAAH

Why can't I start something sweet
like a big umbrella over a small child?
Or start something small
like a kiss?

I need to knock something over, so I can start over.
I am strong enough to shake the planet.
And by the time the shaking's over,
a song will be left standing.

A song will be left standing.
I am so convinced at the typewriter,

my fingers jumping up and down trying to start something.
It's been too long since the last earthquake.

    The first movement comes.

I jump up and down.

(7)

doors open
everyone's home
singing maybe
it's not over

doors open
I hear them slamming
swallowing
for the evening

(82)

terrible boy
telling me I have two faces
one on my head
one on my stomach

terrible girl
asking if I'm pregnant
saying I look like I am
when I am not.

(81)

tell the fire to burn
so you'll be right again

(61)

I like my showers scalding hot
and I like to touch the lids of boiling pots of water.
lately though
I've been getting burned
I've lost a lot of my fingerprints
so I went out and bought some oven mitts
and I'm trying to adjust to my new self.
the unspeakable
opposite
of invincible.

(75)

scratching often switches
the location of my itches

(73)

all the visitors went to the flea market
opened their arms wide
and hugged the life out of secondhand schemes
until nothing was for sale
everything free
the price tags blown back to their original positions
as leaves on the trees
very green
very green
in the shade
lemonade

(22)

if I could take the blood
and put it back on the walls
and take the egg
and put it back in the blood
and take the seed
and slam it into the egg
I would
I would make myself
a mama.

(23)

myself a mama
imagine that
my baby cries for my milk
I make milk, myself
a mama

(64)

it's okay to use candles in daylight
there's no such thing as too bright
I tell myself secrets out loud
the words are invisible, see

it's okay to drink tea in the shower
there's no such thing as too wet
people should make pictures on everything
wet feet make prints on the rug

it's okay to walk up the escalator
I don't want to wait around for the ascension
elevators get stuck between floors
the stairs could stand to be counted

it's okay to close your eyes in the dark
there's no such thing as too black
clouds go somewhere on a clear night
the moon, unseen, knew.

(27)

there are big silent ovals
on the outside of the air
choir mouths
singing O
it's where the wind comes from

(59)

She is risen.
No one will fly higher
no one will enjoy more the loud shouts of angels
or the reverse ocean of the sky.

I got a fever yesterday
because I held too many spirits in me.
They got too crowded and started to sweat me out.

My mama anointed me with Vicks VapoRub
and she put the humidifier on
like a constant genie coming out of the bottle.

And two wooden birds watched me with their right eyes
and a wooden man beat his drum beside me
and a wooden cat kept watch on the other side
and I was held in place by wooden floors
and I was tucked in by wooden doors
and daylight was framed by the wooden window
and if I could see a bit of glory I would
and if I could talk about it anymore I would.

(37)

Turning bad apples
into baked apples,
I am happy
about brown sugar and heat
and look forward
to throwing some ice cream on top.
I love anything
brave enough to melt.

(66)

I cut a record in dreamland
to give the world a taste of its own medicine
I cut patterns for dresses for angels in black fabric
I cut the moon out of cookie dough and bake it at 350 degrees
I cut split ends from my hair and drop them down into a Frisbee
I cut my finger on the thin blade of a wide ruled loose-leaf
I cut a cucumber with a pocketknife into whole half-circles
I cut a moment and watch it sprout
a million minute petals
they pick me up
and carry me
back to the beginning
(once upon a time)
where there are no
sharp
things.

Acknowledgments

Thanks to the editors who placed these poems, sometimes in earlier versions, in the following publications:

Maintenant 5: "contents"
Denver Syntax: "(9)" and "(42)"
Word Riot: "(63)" and "(35)"
In the Shadow of the Mic: Three Decades of Slam Poetry in Pittsburgh: "(35)"
African Voices: "(60)"
The Mom Egg, volume 10: "(10)"
The Stray Branch: "(76)"
Little Red Leaves: "(65)," "(55)," and "(82)"
Mad Rush: "(85)," "(56)," "(86)," "(48)," "(71)," and "(81)"
The Mom Egg, volume 8: "(74)," "(44)," "(75)," and "(61)"
Hip Mama: "(61)"
Spider Magazine: "(84)" (formerly titled "Eggs Over Easy")
The Poetry Super Highway: "(43)" and "(73)"
The Mom Egg, volume 9, and *The Occupy Wall Street Poetry Anthology*: "(83)"
Kweli Journal: "(27)"
Mythium Literary Journal: "(37)," "(40)," "(59)," and "(64)"
Cave Canem Poem of the Week: "(59)"
Mad Rush 2.0: "(66)"

*

96% of these poems were written between 1995 and 1997. In 2009 I attended a poetry workshop for the first time, put the manuscript together, and started submitting. It took 11 more years to be published—25 years after I started writing it.

Sincere thanks to—

the children of San Francisco's Laurel Hill Nursery School, where I was a teacher from 1994 to 1998. The children were also my teachers—their language was the amniotic fluid in which these early poems grew.

the Black and Brown communities and poetry teachers, who, although unknown to me at the time these poems were written, made me into the poet and author I am today—VONA: Willie Perdomo and Suheir Hammad; Hurston/Wright Writers Week: Tyehimba Jess; Callaloo Creative Writing Workshops: Vievee Francis and Gregory Pardlo; Cave Canem: Toi Derricotte, Cornelius Eady, Terrance Hayes, Carl Phillips, Claudia Rankine, Natasha Trethewey, Chris Abani, Lyrae Van Clief-Stefanon, Tim Seibels, Patricia Smith, Amber Flora Thomas, and Willie Perdomo (again!); CAAPP: Sonia Sanchez.

the host of people who helped me, and select poems, come to life on stages, including—Jennifer Joseph (Poetry Above Paradise—my first featured reading), Bob Booker, Amanda Gilby, Kat Georges, Joseph Hall, Puma Perl, Marjorie Tesser; Steel City Slam: Alaina Dopico, Brian Francis, William James, and Adriana Ramirez; New Hazlett Theater CSA: René Conrad, Monty Stevens Kane, Andy Ostrowski, Mark Staley, and Stephanie Mayer-Staley.

and to Elmaz Abinader, Renée Alberts, Harry Alter, Aida Ashouri, S. Erin Batiste, Oscar Bermeo, Danielle Brown, Amalia Bueno, Sheila Carter-Jones, Danielle Chiotti, Aimee DeFoe, Bill Delaney, Alyss Dixson, Greg Horne, Vanessa Huang, Diem Jones, Miriam Ching Yoon Louie, Maya Marshall, Janine Mogannam, Ladan Osman, Deesha Philyaw, Kathy Z. Price, Amir Rabiyah, Erik Rader, Darlene Rodrigues, Lauren Russell, Rose M. Smith, L'Oreal Snell, Richard St. John, Gabrielle Strong, Mariahadesse Ekere Tallie, Cedric Tillman, Jonnie Viakley, Andrea Walls, Maya Washington, Wayno, R. Weis, Michelle Whittaker, Sue Wrbican, Sue Abramson and each of my photography teachers and classmates at Pittsburgh Filmmakers (back in the Oakland Avenue days), and my blurb contributors for delivering in a pandemic.

Special thanks to Monty Stevens Kane, Abby Stevens Kane, my parents, Tim Stevens, Marcus Stevens, Jennifer Andrade, Arlene Andrade, Rachel Nelson, Lisa Panepinto, Aurelia Lavalee and the Spuyten Duyvil editorial team, and You.

In hope for Tonee Turner.

In honor of CBJ, JGJ, ACK, MSM, JSS, and GHS.

KELLI STEVENS KANE is a poet, playwright, oral historian, and accountant. She's a Cave Canem Fellow, an August Wilson Center Fellow, and a recipient of Advancing Black Arts in Pittsburgh grants from The Pittsburgh Foundation. She's studied at VONA, Hurston/Wright, and Callaloo. Kane's poems have appeared in *North American Review*, *Little Patuxent Review*, *Under a Warm Green Linden*, *Painted Bride Quarterly*, and *Split This Rock*. She's read her poetry and oral history and performed her one woman show, *Big George*, nationally. This is her first book. For more information visit www.kellistevenskane.com.